The Messiah

Printed in the U S A

INTRODUCTORY NOTE

THE MESSIAH, Handel's most successful and best-known oratorio, was composed in the year 1741 in twenty-four days, from August the 22d to September the 14th It was first performed at a concert given for charitable purposes at Dublin, Ireland, on April the 13th, 1742, Handel conducting the performance in person

According to the historical evidence, Handel knew that the Dublin orchestral and choral resources were by no means on a par with those of London, and was markedly influenced by this circumstance in the composition of his work In his choruses he did not go beyond four-part writing, and kept his orchestra within the most modest limits, so that no instrument except violin and trumpet plays a solo part, and oboe and bassoon do not appear at all in the score, although these instruments participated in the performance, as was proved by a later discovery of orchestra-parts written for both Thereafter Handel, beginning with March the 23d, 1743, brought out *The Messiah* every year in London with great applause, in the course of time he made various alterations in certain numbers, set several new ones to music, transcribed a few arias for different voices, but left the work as a whole unchanged, both vocally and instrumentally, from its original form, thus bearing witness that, despite its limitations, this primitive conception of the work was likewise the enduring one

As the centuries have passed, a considerable number of vocal scores have, of course, been made after Handel's partition, notably that by Dr Clarke (Whitfield-Clarke, 1809), and a later one by Vincent Novello Their value, however, was more or less doubtful, their character being rather that of transcriptions in pianoforte style, with not infrequent arbitrary or capricious aberrations, than a faithful and exact reduction of the orchestral score Neither have the more recent editions of vocal scores based on the Mozart orchestra score, with its many contrapuntal charms, quite fulfilled expectations, as they materially increased the difficulty of the piano part

Hence, a vocal score which should be in every way reliable and practical has become a matter of prime necessity The present edition agrees at every point with Handel's original score, as it follows the facsimile edition of this latter with most careful exactitude Slight deviations from the original, which in the course of many years have obtained almost traditional authority, are inserted in small notes in every case, the professional artist being left free to employ them or not, at his discretion

With regard to the performance of this grand work by chorus and soloists, much of importance might be said, but this would lead too far afield, and we shall, therefore, confine ourselves to the matters of chiefest concern The direction of the choruses, which in our Master's works are for the most part peculiarly prominent in their monumental character, will naturally be entrusted to competent chorus conductors, who will care for crystalling precision of execution and a clear, logical conception, and who are responsible for these points

The interpretation of their parts by the soloists is a different affair Here we confront the weighty question "May the soloist proceed subjectively, or must he proceed objectively?" Probably the best answer to this crucial query is found in a passage from the unrivalled work of an authority in this province, namely, "Die Lehre von der vokalen Ornamentik des 17 und 18 Jahrhunderts," by Dr Hugo Goldschmidt He writes "The essence of reproduction, to feel and re-create that which was felt and imparted by the creator, does not exclude —within natural limitations—the assertion of creative power The modern theory of æsthetics founded by Lipps rightly proceeds from the idea, that the interpreting artist creates, in a sense, the work anew With his gradual penetration of the art-work he creates new values, which are of the highest importance for art, because, without them, the creations of the great masters are only so much writing, and thus remain sealed to enjoyment But the interpreter's work is no mere execution, comparable, let us say, to that of the builder who transmutes the architect's plans into material reality His task is rather to seize the vital conception of the art-work, to blend it with his own ego and the views of his period, and thus to imbue it with life and effectiveness Whether singer or instrumentalist, he is a child of his time His artistry is a product of its mental culture It develops and changes with the evolution of artistic requirements His formative and emotional powers are derived from the spirit of the epoch to which he belongs. Consequently, we shall always approach the art-productions of earlier times through the medium of our own spiritual and emotional nature. It follows, that the domain which such artistic reproduction may open to us, although of great extent, and as broad in scope as the points of contact with modern sensibility can reach, will be dependent in any given period on a constantly shifting relation to the treasures of former ages. The genuine, great masterworks of the past retain their importance; they are immortal; but our relations to them are not constant, and change with the changing impressionability of the times. We hear the works of these past-masters of former centuries—of Palestrina, Gabrieli, Händel and Bach, yes, even of Mozart and Beethoven—with other ears than our forefathers, or even than our grandfathers. What we have experienced since their time, whatever we have wrested to our eternal gain, this it is which sounds in those works to our ears. Much that charmed former generations has no effect in ours; so much is part and parcel of the time which gave it birth, and decays with its passing. Only what is exalted over time and place remains as eternal gain; and here, again, another generation finds new treasures that earlier ones passed by unheeding. This is the unfailing criterion of true greatness, that its creations continually beget ever-new, ever-changing values, that they bring to each successive generation new revelations. Consider the history of Händel's art. The eighteenth century, in its latter half, admired it in the form of arrangements by contemporaries, those by Mozart and Hiller. Our present-day musical interpretation—on Dr. Chrysander's initiative—has gone back to the historically authenticated form, and disclosed to us the true Händel in his full grandeur. But it owes its success, not to a recognition that things must be so because Händel would have them so, but because they appeal more directly to our sense and feeling than do the arrangements of the eighteenth and nineteenth centuries."

Such are the pregnant and weighty pronouncements of an experienced man, deeply versed in musico-historical lore and research. They should be of the highest value to the serious artist.

Here a word shall be said touching the employment of the appoggiaturas in the recitatives and (in isolated cases) also in the arias. They are, of course, not given in this edition, or indicated only very infrequently.

The Appoggiatura, in Händel's works, must be treated with the utmost caution and nicest discrimination. It should never be regarded as a mere ornament, but always fulfil some declamatory, melodic or harmonic function. Do not lose sight of the fact, that the appoggiatura lends greater elasticity and emphasis to the flow of melody and declamation, and also to the musical expression; at the same time, one cannot be too careful not to introduce it too often, for this would doubtless produce an unpleasing and inadmissible monotony instead of enhancing the effect.

According to historical evidence, Händel permitted his singers to employ appoggiaturas, and even melismata and cadences, in the arias of his oratorios; he invariably insisted, however, that they should not be mere embellishments serving simply for outward display of vocal effect, but calculated to promote the melodic flow and declamatory expression, and must, consequently, possess musical meaning and value. Mistakes in the use of these ornaments can be prevented only by a thorough knowledge of the development of vocal embellishments, a certain penetration into the spirit of Händel's oratorios, and a refined taste in matters pertaining to musical æsthetics.

The Appoggiatura is unquestionably the most important and most frequently employed among the ornaments, and a few general observations concerning the principles involved can hardly fail to be welcome; more especially as they are accompanied by a number of practical illustrations.

An appoggiatura is in place where its introduction brings about a diatonic succession, and more particularly across the bar, in order to avoid the leap of a third; for example in No. 5, page 26:

come to His temple   =   come to His temple

and similarly within the boundaries of one measure, as in No. 19, page 94:

blind be o-pen'd   =   blind be o-pen'd

These latter must, however, be introduced with careful discrimination; otherwise appoggiaturas of this sort are very apt to produce a feeling of monotony and an interruption of the melodic flow. Another species of appoggiatura which may be used very effectively is the leap to the fourth below; this occurs both in the midst of a measure No. 19, page 94):

iv

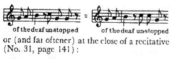

of the deaf unstopped   of the deaf unstopped

or (and far oftener) at the close of a recitative (No. 31, page 141):

was He stricken.   was He stricken.

Besides these, the leap of the appoggiatura to the sixth below is occasionally met with (No. 2, page 9):

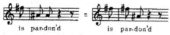

is par-don'd   is par-don'd

The appoggiatura leading upward by a step is seldom or never employed; leading up by a leap it is very successfully applied in certain cases, for example in No. 2, page 9:

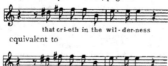

that cri-eth in the wil-der-ness

equivalent to

that cri-eth in the wil-der-ness

or No. 8, page 47:

Em-man-u-el   Em-man-u-el

Great discretion and sound judgment are, however, very necessary for governing the employment of this upward-leaping appoggiatura; for if, in a quite analogous situation, as shown in No. 5, page 25:

the   dry land,   all na-tions,   I'll

the appoggiatura were introduced at the similar points:

the   dry land,   all na-tions,   I'll

this would be, not simply a regrettably blunder, but a total misinterpretation of this important passage.

Illustrations of this kind show most convincingly how important it is that the singer should treat each case, as it arises, logically and

discreetly, and how the appoggiature, in apparently analogous situations, must sometimes be employed and at other avoided. The finest and most striking examples of this description, in our opinion, are those given by Händel in *The Messiah* on page 129 (No. 29): "Thy rebuke hath broken His heart," and on page 140 (No. 30): "Behold, and see." These two numbers, which are among the most beautiful, sublime and affecting of all that Händel has given us in his oratorios, and which convey a sense of mournful, hopeless anxiety in a manner of almost unparalleled realism, should be attentively studied by every oratorio-singer who truly loves his art.

We seize this occasion to direct attention to another important matter, which ought to be mentioned, if for no other reason, because it is unnoticed in all the other vocal scores. We refer to the chorus "Glory to God!" page 82 (No. 17). Here Händel inserted in his original score the following phrase: "da lontano e un poco piano" (as from a distance, and rather softly); and only thus should this chorus be performed. It appears to us that, relying on Händel's directions for the dynamics of this number, there can be no doubt that he intended a gradual approach (augmentation) of this solemn chant, as of an increasingly urgent, divinely inspired announcement, followed by an equally gradual *decrescendo* withdrawal. Supporting evidence is found in the postlude, which, after a grand *fortissimo* climax of the chorus, dies away to a whispered *pianissimo*,— The authenticity of the above reading has occasionally been called in question, with argument both in speech and writing; but such questioning can rest only on a lack of acquaintance—or an inexact acquaintance—with Händel's original score. So, in order to settle this important point definitely, we publish at the beginning of this edition a facsimile of the first page of this chorus from Händel's original manuscript, which should suffice to set the question at rest forever.

In our edition the greatest care has also been bestowed upon the word-text, and each number provided with a correct reference to the corresponding section in the Bible.

We can, therefore, publish this edition with the consciousness that it has been prepared with the thoroughness and reverent care due to this eternally beautiful masterwork.

MAX SPICKER.

New York, March, 1912.

THE MESSIAH

PART I

1 OVERTURE

2 RECIT *Accompanied* (TENOR)

Comfort ye, comfort ye my people, saith your God, speak ye comfortably to Jerusalem, and cry unto her, that her warfare is accomplishèd, that her iniquity is pardoned

The voice of him that crieth in the wilderness, Prepare ye the way of the Lord, make straight in the desert a highway for our God

3 AIR (TENOR)

Every valley shall be exalted, and every mountain and hill made low, the crooked straight, and the rough places plain

4 CHORUS

And the glory of the Lord shall be revealèd, and all flesh shall see it together, for the mouth of the Lord hath spoken it

5 RECIT *Accompanied* (BASS)

Thus saith the Lord of Hosts —Yet once a little while and I will shake the heavens, and the earth, the sea, and the dry land, and I will shake all nations, and the desire of all nations shall come

The Lord, whom ye seek, shall suddenly come to his temple, even the messenger of the covenant, whom ye delight in, Behold, He shall come, saith the Lord of Hosts

6 AIR (BASS)

But who may abide the day of His coming, and who shall stand when He appeareth?

For He is like a refiner's fire

7 CHORUS

And He shall purify the sons of Levi, that they may offer unto the Lord an offering in righteousness

8 RECIT (ALTO)

Behold, a virgin shall conceive, and bear a Son, and shall call his name EMMANUEL God with us

9 AIR (ALTO) AND CHORUS

O thou that tellest good tidings to Zion, get thee up into the high mountain, O thou that tellest good tidings to Jerusalem, lift up thy voice with strength, lift it up, be not afraid, say unto the cities of Judah, Behold your God!

Arise, shine, for thy light is come, and the glory of the Lord is risen upon thee

10 RECIT *Accompanied* (BASS)

For, behold, darkness shall cover the earth, and gross darkness the people, but the Lord shall arise upon thee, and His glory shall be seen upon thee, and the Gentiles shall come to thy light, and kings to the brightness of thy rising

11 AIR (BASS)

The people that walked in darkness have seen a great light and they that dwell in the land of the shadow of death, upon them hath the light shined

12 CHORUS

For unto us a Child is born, unto us a Son is given, and the government shall be upon His shoulder and His name shall be called Wonderful, Counsellor, the Mighty God, the Everlasting Father, the Prince of Peace

13 PASTORAL SYMPHONY

14 RECIT (SOPRANO)

There were shepherds abiding in the field, keeping watch over their flocks by night

RECIT *Accompanied* (SOPRANO)

And lo! the angel of the Lord came upon them, and the glory of the Lord shone round about them, and they were sore afraid

15 RECIT (SOPRANO)

And the angel said unto them, Fear not, for, behold, I bring you good tidings of great joy, which shall be to all people

For unto you is born this day in the city of David a Saviour, which is Christ the Lord

16 RECIT *Accompanied* (Soprano)

And suddenly there was with the angel a multitude of the heavenly host praising God, and saying

17 CHORUS

Glory to God in the highest, and peace on earth, good will towards men

18 AIR (Soprano)

Rejoice greatly, O daughter of Zion, Shout, O daughter of Jerusalem behold, thy king cometh unto thee

He is the righteous Saviour, and He shall speak peace unto the heathen

19 RECIT (Alto)

Then shall the eyes of the blind be opened, and the ears of the deaf unstoppèd, then shall the lame man leap as an hart, and the tongue of the dumb shall sing

20 AIR (Alto)

He shall feed His flock like a shepherd, and He shall gather the lambs with His arm, and carry them in His bosom, and gently lead those that are with young

AIR (Soprano)

Come unto Him, all ye that labour and are heavy laden, and He shall give you rest

Take His yoke upon you, and learn of Him, for He is meek and lowly of heart and ye shall find rest unto your souls

21 CHORUS

His yoke is easy and His burthen is light

PART II

22 CHORUS

Behold the Lamb of God, that taketh away the sins of the world

23 AIR (Alto)

He was despisèd and rejected of men a man of sorrows, and acquainted with grief

*[He gave His back to the smiters, and His cheeks to them that plucked off the hair He hid not His face from shame and spitting]

24 CHORUS

Surely He hath borne our griefs, and carried our sorrows, He was wounded for our transgressions, He was bruised for our iniquities, the chastisement of our peace was upon Him

25 CHORUS

And with His stripes we are healèd

26 CHORUS

All we like sheep have gone astray, we have turnèd every one to his own way, and the Lord hath laid on Him the iniquity of us all

*The latter part of this Air is usually omitted

27 RECIT *Accompanied* (Tenor)

All they that see Him, laugh Him to scorn, they shoot out their lips, and shake their heads, saying —

28 CHORUS

He trusted in God that He would deliver Him, let Him deliver Him, if He delight in Him

29 RECIT *Accompanied* (Tenor)

Thy rebuke hath broken His heart, He is full of heaviness He looked for some to have pity on Him, but there was no man, neither found He any to comfort Him

30 AIR (Tenor)

Behold, and see if there be any sorrow like unto His sorrow

31 RECIT *Accompanied* (Tenor)

He was cut off out of the land of the living for the transgression of Thy people was He stricken

32 AIR (Tenor)

But Thou didst not leave His soul in hell, nor didst Thou suffer Thy Holy One to see corruption

33 CHORUS

Lift up your heads, O ye gates, and be ye lift up, ye everlasting doors, and the King of glory shall come in

Who is the King of glory? The Lord strong and mighty, the Lord mighty in battle

Lift up your heads, O ye gates, and be ye lift up, ye everlasting doors, and the King of glory shall come in

Who is the King of glory? The Lord of Hosts, He is the King of glory

34 RECIT (Tenor)

Unto which of the angels said He at any time, Thou art my Son, this day have I begotten Thee?

35 CHORUS

Let all the angels of God worship Him

36 AIR* (Bass)

[Thou art gone up on high, Thou hast led captivity captive, and received gifts for men, yea, even for Thine enemies, that the Lord God might dwell among them]

37 CHORUS

The Lord gave the word great was the company of the preachers

38 AIR (Soprano)

How beautiful are the feet of them that preach the gospel of peace, and bring glad tidings of good things

39 CHORUS

Their sound is gone out into all lands, and their words unto the ends of the world

40 AIR (Bass)

Why do the nations so furiously rage together? [and] why do the people imagine a vain thing?

The kings of the earth rise up, and the rulers take counsel together against the Lord, and against His Anointed

41 CHORUS

Let us break their bonds asunder, and cast away their yokes from us

42 RECIT (Tenor)

He that dwelleth in heaven shall laugh them to scorn the Lord shall have them in derision

43 AIR (Tenor)

Thou shalt break them with a rod of iron; Thou shalt dash them in pieces like a potter's vessel

44 CHORUS

HALLELUJAH! for the Lord God omnipotent reigneth

The kingdom of this world is become the kingdom of our Lord, and of His Christ and He shall reign for ever and ever

KING OF KINGS, AND LORD OF LORDS, HAL-LELUJAH!

PART III

45 AIR (Soprano)

I know that my Redeemer liveth, and that He shall stand at the latter day upon the earth

And though worms destroy this body, yet in my flesh shall I see God

For now is Christ risen from the dead, the first-fruits of them that sleep

*This air is usually omitted

46 CHORUS

Since by man came death, by man came also the resurrection of the dead For as in Adam all die, even so in Christ shall all be made alive

47 RECIT Accompanied (Bass)

Behold, I tell you a mystery We shall not all

sleep, but we shall all be changed in a moment, in a twinkling of an eye, at the last trumpet

48 AIR (Bass)

The trumpet shall sound, and the dead shall be raised in corruptible, and we shall be changed

*[For this corruptible must put on incorruption, and this mortal must put on immortality]

49 RECIT † (Alto)

Then shall be brought to pass the saying that is written Death is swallowed up in victory

50 DUET (Alto and Tenor)

O death, where is thy sting? O grave, where is thy victory? The sting of death is sin, and the strength of sin is the law

51 CHORUS

But thanks be to God, who giveth us the victory through our Lord Jesus Christ

52 AIR (Soprano)

If God be for us, who can be against us? who shall lay any thing to the charge of God's elect? It is God that justifieth, who is he that condemneth?

It is Christ that died, yea, rather, that is risen again, who is at the right hand of God, who makes intercession for us

53 CHORUS

Worthy is the Lamb that was slain, and hath redeemed us to God by His blood, to receive power, and riches, and wisdom, and strength, and honour, and glory, and blessing

Blessing and honour, glory and power, be unto Him that sitteth upon the throne, and unto the Lamb, for ever and ever
Amen

*The latter part of this Air is usually omitted
†This and the three following pieces are sometimes omitted

INDEX

PART I

PART II

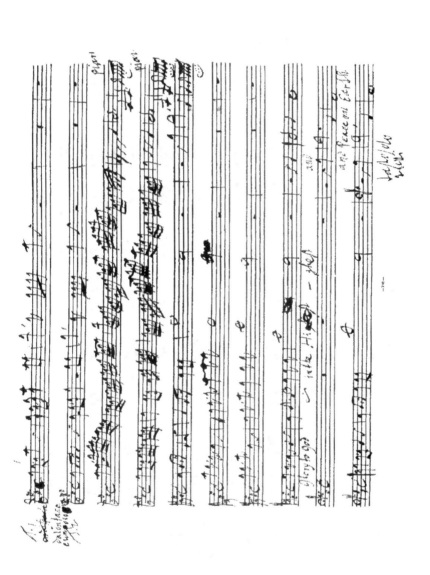

THE MESSIAH

PART I

Nº 1. – OVERTURE

G. F. Händel

22945 X

Nº 2.–RECITATIVE FOR TENOR

"COMFORT YE MY PEOPLE"

Isaiah xl. 1-3

Larghetto e piano (♪ = 80)

TENOR SOLO

Com-fort ye, com - - fort ye ___ my peo-ple, com - fort ye,

com - - fort ye my peo-ple,

22945

saith your God,   saith your God;

speak ye com-fort-a-bly to   Je - ru - sa-lem,   speak ye

com-fort-a-bly to   Je - ru - sa-lem,   and cry un-to her that her

B

war - fare,   her   war - fare is ac-complished,   that her in-

Original orchestral score has:

cry un-to her   is ac-com-plish'd

22945

9

i - qui - ty is par-don'd, that her in - i - qui - ty is par -

don'd.

mf

C

The voice of him that crieth in the wilderness, Pre-pare ye the way of the

Lord, make straight in the desert a high-way for our God.

45

Nº 3.– AIR FOR TENOR
"EVERY VALLEY SHALL BE EXALTED"

Isaiah xl: 4

the crook-ed straight, and the rough plac-es

plain, _____ the crook-ed

straight, the crook - ed straight, and rough plac-es plain, _____

cresc.

p

simile

and the rough plac-es plain.

C

Ev-'ry val-ley,   ev-'ry val-ley

shall be ex-alt-

-ed,

22945

D

ev -'ry val-ley, ev -'ry val-ley shall be ex-alt -

- ed, and ev'ry moun-tain and

hill made low; the crook-ed straight, the

crook-ed straight, the crook-ed straight, and the rough plac-es plain,

and the rough plac-es plain, and the rough plac-es

plain, _____ the crook-ed straight,

ad lib. E

and the rough plac - es plain.

colla voce in tempo

senza Ped.

Nº 4. – CHORUS

"AND THE GLORY OF THE LORD"

Isaiah xl: 5

*) According to the original score

22945

22945

glo - ry, the glo - ry of the Lord shall be re - veal - ed,

glo - ry, the glo - ry of the Lord shall be re - veal - ed,

glo - ry, the glo - ry of the Lord shall be re-veal - ed,

glo - ry, the glo - ry of the Lord shall be re - veal - ed,

mf and all flesh shall

see it to - geth-er,

mf and all flesh shall see it to - geth-er;

Nº 5. – RECITATIVE FOR BASS

"THUS SAITH THE LORD"

of all na - tions shall come.

B *Recit.*

The Lord whom ye seek shall suddenly come to His tem-ple, ev'n the

mes-sen-ger of the cov - e -nant, whom ye de -light in;

Be-hold, he shall come, saith the Lord of Hosts.

Nº 6. – AIR FOR BASS

"But who may abide the day of His coming?"

Malachi III: 2

Larghetto (♪ = 88)

Bass Solo **A**

But who may a-

bide the day of His com-ing? and who shall stand when

He__ ap - pear-eth? who shall __ stand when

22945

B

He ap - pear-eth? But who may a - bide, but

who may a - bide the day of His com-ing? and

who shall stand when He ap - - pear-eth?

C

and who shall stand when

He ap - pear - - - - - -

- - - eth?   when _____ He ap - pear - -

D

eth?

Prestissimo ($\mathjot{d}$ = 138)

_pp_

cresc.   _f_

For   He   is   like _____ a   re -

fin - - - er's _____ fire, _____

for He is like _____ a re-

fin - - - - - - - - - - -

- - - - - er's _____ fire.

E

Who shall stand when He ap-

pear - eth? For He is like a re-

fin - - - - - - - - - - er's fire, for

He is like a re - fin - - - - - -

- - er's fire,

and who shall stand when He ap - pear-eth?

cresc.

colla voce

fire, and who shall stand when He,

when He ap - -pear-eth? and who shall

stand when He ap -

pear - eth? For He is

like a re - fin - - - - er's

I Adagio

---ers fire,   for He is like a re - fin - ers

Prestissimo

fire.

Nº 7.– CHORUS

"AND HE SHALL PURIFY"

Malachi iii: 3

38

22945

42

12945

44

22945

un - - to the Lord an of - fer - ing in right - eous -

un - - to the Lord an of - fer - ing in right - - eous -

un - - to the Lord an of - fer - ing in right - - eous -

un - - to the Lord an of - fer - ing in right - - eous -

ness, in right - eous - ness.

ness, in right-eous - ness.

ness, in right-eous - ness.

ness, in right - eous - ness.

mf

№ 8.– RECITATIVE FOR ALTO
"BEHOLD! A VIRGIN SHALL CONCEIVE"

Isaiah vii: 14.—Matt. i: 23

Be-hold! a vir-gin shall con-ceive, and bear a son, and shall call his name Em - man - u - el: God with us.

№ 9.– AIR FOR ALTO, AND CHORUS
"O THOU THAT TELLEST GOOD TIDINGS TO ZION"

Isaiah xl: 9

Andante (♩ = 144)

22945

48

22945

un-to the cit-ies of Ju - - dah, Be-

hold ___ your God! ___ be - hold your God! ___

be - hold your God!

E

O

thou that tell-est good ti-dings to Zi - on,

22945

a - rise, shine, for thy light is come;

a - rise, a -

rise,___ a - rise, shine, for thy light is come,

and the glo -

- ry of the Lord, the

CHORUS

58

22945

22945

Nº 10.– RECITATIVE FOR BASS
"FOR BEHOLD, DARKNESS SHALL COVER THE EARTH"

Isaiah lx: 2,3

Andante larghetto (♪ = 72)

For be-hold, dark-ness shall cov - er the earth, and gross dark - ness the peo-ple, and gross dark - ness the peo-ple:

but the Lord shall a - rise

up - on thee, and His

glo - - - - ry shall be seen up - on thee, and His

glo - - ry shall be seen up - on thee. And the Gentiles shall

come to thy light, and kings to the brightness of thy ris - ing.

Nº 11.– AIR FOR BASS
"THE PEOPLE THAT WALKED IN DARKNESS"

Isaiah ix: 2

walk-ed in darkness have seen a great light,

B

the peo-ple that walk-ed, that walk-ed in dark-ness, that

walk-ed in dark - ness, the peo-ple that walk-ed in dark - -

- - - - ness have seen a great light, have seen a great light,

- a great light, _____ have seen a great light:

and

they that dwell,— that dwell in the land of the shad - - -

- - ow of death,— and

they that dwell, that dwell in the land,— that dwell in the land of the

shad-ow of death,— up -

Nº 12. – CHORUS

"For unto us a Child is born"

Isaiah ix: 6

68

22945

74

The might-y God, The ev-er-last-ing Fa-ther, The Prince of Peace, The

The might-y God, The ev-er-last-ing Fa-ther, The Prince of Peace, The

The might-y God, The ev-er-last-ing Fa-ther, The Prince of Peace, The

The might-y God, The ev-er-last-ing Fa-ther, The Prince of Peace, The

ev-er-last-ing Father, The Prince of Peace.

ev-er-last-ing Fa-ther, The Prince of Peace.

ev-er-last-ing Fa-ther, The Prince of Peace.

ev-er-last-ing Fa-ther, The Prince of Peace.

Nº 13.
PASTORAL SYMPHONY

№ 14.– RECITATIVE FOR SOPRANO
"THERE WERE SHEPHERDS ABIDING IN THE FIELD"

RECITATIVE FOR SOPRANO
"AND LO! THE ANGEL OF THE LORD CAME UPON THEM"

Nº 15. – RECITATIVE FOR SOPRANO
"AND THE ANGEL SAID UNTO THEM"

Luke ii : 10,11

And the an-gel said un-to them, Fear not: for be-

hold, I bring you good ti-dings of great joy, which shall

be to all peo-ple. For un-to you is born this

day in the cit-y of Da-vid a Sav-iour, which is Christ the Lord.

Nº 16. – RECITATIVE FOR SOPRANO

"AND SUDDENLY THERE WAS WITH THE ANGEL"

Luke ii: 13

And sud-den-ly there was with the

an-gel a mul-ti-tude of the heav'nly host

prais-ing God, and say - - ing:

22945

Nº 17. – CHORUS
"GLORY TO GOD"

Luke II:14

*)Original scor nas b e de lontano e un poco piano" (as from a distance, and rather softly)

22945

Nº 18. – AIR FOR SOPRANO

"REJOICE GREATLY, O DAUGHTER OF ZION!"

Zechariah ix: 9,10

O daugh-ter of Zi-on! re-joice, _____ re-joice,

re-joice!

B

O daugh-ter of Zi-on! Re - joice _____ great-ly,

shout, _____ O daugh-ter of Je-ru-sa-lem: be-

Be-hold, thy king com-eth un - to thee, re-joice,

re-joice

and shout, shout, shout, shout, re-joice

greatly,

G

re-joice greatly, O daugh-ter of Zi - on! shout,

O daugh-ter of Je - - ru - sa-lem! Be-hold, thy

king com-eth un - - to thee, be-hold, thy king com-eth un - to

ad lib.

colla voce

thee.

p

Nº 19. – RECITATIVE FOR ALTO
"THEN SHALL THE EYES OF THE BLIND BE OPENED"

Isaiah xxxv: 5,6

Then shall the eyes of the blind be open'd, and the ears of the deaf un-stopped. Then shall the lame man leap as an hart, and the tongue of the dumb shall sing.

*) In the original score, this is given to the Soprano, in the key of G. But, as the first part of Nº 20 is usually sung by a Contralto, it is better that the Recitative should be sung by the same voice.

Nº 20. – AIR FOR ALTO
"HE SHALL FEED HIS FLOCK LIKE A SHEPHERD"

Isaiah xl: 11 - Matt. xl: 28, 29

Larghetto, e piano (♩=112)

He shall feed His flock like a shep - - herd, and He shall ga - ther the lambs with His arm, with His arm,

*) Often sung thus

He shall feed His flock

SOPRANO SOLO

*) C   **)

Come un - to — Him, all ye that la - bour, come

un - to — Him, ye that are — heav-y la - den, — and He will give you rest.

*)   **)

Come un - to — Him, — all ye that la - bour, come

un - to — Him, — ye that are heav-y la - den, — and He will give you rest.

cresc.

D

Take His yoke up-on you, and learn — of Him, for

*) Often sung thus: Come — un - to Him, **) come un - to Him, ye that are heav - y

He— is— meek— and low-ly of heart, and ye—shall find rest,— and

ye shall find rest un - to— your souls.

E

Take His yoke up-on you, and learn of Him, for He— is— meek— and

low-ly of heart, and ye shall find rest, and ye shall find rest un - to—your souls.

22945

Nº 21. – CHORUS

"HIS YOKE IS EASY, AND HIS BURTHEN IS LIGHT"

100

22945

*) Original score has in bass here:

END OF PART I

PART II

Nº 22. – CHORUS
"Behold the Lamb of God"

John 1: 29

*) Original score has here: and here **)

*) Original score:

№ 23. – AIR FOR ALTO
"HE WAS DESPISED"

Isaiah liii: 3; l: 6

*) Original score

a man of sor- -rows, and ac-quainted with grief, ___

___ a man of sor-rows, and ac-quainted with grief.

He

was des-pis-ed, re-ject-ed, He was des-

*) Original score has *a♭* here, but usually *a♮* is sung instead.

pis- ed and re-ject-ed of men; a man of sorrows, and acquainted with
grief, _____ a man of sor-rows, and ac- quaint-ed with grief.
He was despis -ed, re-ject-ed; a man of
sorrows, and acquainted with grief, and acquainted with grief,
a man of sorrows, and ac-quainted with grief.

hair, and his cheeks to them that plucked off the

hair: He hid not His face from shame and

spit-ting, He hid not His face from shame,——

from shame,—— He hid not His

face from shame,—— from shame and spitting.

Nº 24. – CHORUS
"SURELY HE HATH BORNE OUR GRIEFS"

Isaiah liii: **4, 5**

Largo e staccato (♪ = 72)

Nº 25. – CHORUS

"AND WITH HIS STRIPES WE ARE HEALED"

Isaiah IIII: **5**

Nº 26. – CHORUS

"ALL WE LIKE SHEEP HAVE GONE ASTRAY"

126

128

22945

130

№ 27. – RECITATIVE FOR TENOR

"ALL THEY THAT SEE HIM, LAUGH HIM TO SCORN"

Psalm xxii: 7

Larghetto (♪ = 80)

TENOR SOLO

All they that see Him, laugh Him to scorn; they shoot out their lips, and shake their heads, say - ing:

Nº 28. – CHORUS

"He trusted in God that He would deliver Him"

134

№ 29. - RECITATIVE FOR TENOR

"THY REBUKE HATH BROKEN HIS HEART"

Psalm lxix: 20

Largo

Nº 30. – AIR FOR TENOR

"BEHOLD, AND SEE IF THERE BE ANY SORROW"

Lamentations 1: 12

Nọ 31. - RECITATIVE FOR TENOR

"HE WAS CUT OFF OUT OF THE LAND OF THE LIVING"

Isaiah lIII: 8

Nọ 32. - AIR FOR TENOR

"BUT THOU DIDST NOT LEAVE HIS SOUL IN HELL"

Psalm xvi: 10

Andante larghetto ($\bullet$ = 108)

*) This is according to Händel's score; other editions have not t appogy ura

142

soul in ___ hell, nor didst ___ Thou suf-fer, nor didst Thou suf-fer Thy

Ho - ly ___ One to see cor-rup-tion.

But Thou didst not leave His

soul in hell, Thou didst not leave, Thou didst not leave His

soul in hell, nor didst Thou suf-fer Thy

Ho - ly One   to see cor-rup-tion,   nor didst Thou suf-fer, nor

didst Thou suf-fer Thy Ho - ly One   to see cor - rup - tion,

nor didst Thou suf-fer, nor didst Thou suf-fer Thy Ho - ly One, Thy

Ho - ly One   to see cor-rup-tion,

Nº 33. – CHORUS

"LIFT UP YOUR HEADS, O YE GATES"

Psalm xxiv: 7-10

G. F. Händel

A tempo ordinario (♩ = 76)

*) Händel's sco . . . . become tradi-
tional, howeve . . . . h b . . .

Printed in the U. S. A.

*) Nº 34. – RECITATIVE FOR TENOR

"Unto which of the angels said He"

*) Nº 35. – CHORUS

"Let all the angels of God worship Him"

+) Generally omitted

*) N⁰ 36. – AIR FOR BASS

"Thou art gone up on high" ²

*) Generally omitted.

e - - ven for Thine en - - - - e - mies,

yea, e - ven for_____ Thine en - e - mies,

that the Lord

God might dwell__ a - mong them, that the Lord God might dwell,_____

might dwell a-mong them.

Thou art gone up on high, Thou art gone up on high, Thou hast

led cap-tiv - i - ty cap-tive, Thou hast led cap-tiv - i - ty cap-tive,

and re - ceiv - ed gifts for men; yea, e - ven

for Thine en - - - - - - - - -

God might dwell a- - mong them, might dwell

a - mong

them, that the Lord God might dwell a-mong them.

Nº 37. – CHORUS

"The Lord gave the word"

Psalm lxviii: 11

"How beautiful are the feet of them"

Romans x: 15

Larghetto (♪ = 104)

Soprano Solo

How beau-ti-ful are the feet of them that preach the gos-pel of peace, how beau-ti-ful are the feet, how beau-ti-ful are the feet of them that preach the gos-pel of peace, how beau-ti-ful are the feet of them that

preach the gos-pel of peace, and bring glad ti - - -dings, and
bring glad ti - - -dings, glad ti - dings of good things, and

B

bring glad ti - -dings, glad tidings of good things, and bring glad tidings, glad
ti-dings of good things, glad tidings of good things!

Nº 39. – CHORUS

"THEIR SOUND IS GONE OUT INTO ALL LANDS"

Nº40 – AIR FOR BASS

"WHY DO THE NATIONS SO FURIOUSLY RAGE TOGETHER?"

Psalm ii: 1,2

A Bass Solo

Why do the na - - tions so fu - rious-ly rage to - -geth - er? why do the peo - -ple im - a - gine a vain thing? Why do the na - - tions

rage

fu-rious-ly to - geth - er?   why

do   the   peo - ple   in - a - - - - - - - - - -

- - - - - - - - - gine a vain

peo-ple im- -a- -gine a vain

thing? Why do the na- -tions

rage

so furiously to-gether, so furiously to-geth-er? and

why do the peo-ple im- -a- -gine a vain

thing? im - a - - - - gine a

-gine a vain thing? and

why do the peo-ple im- -a- gine a vain

D

thing?

The kings of the earth rise up, and the rul- -ers take coun - sel to - geth- -er, take

coun - sel, take

coun - sel to-geth-er againstthe Lord, and a -

gainst... His an - oint - - - - - -

- - - ed, a - gainst the Lord and His an -

oint - - - - - - - - ed.

Nº 41.- CHORUS
"LET US BREAK THEIR BONDS ASUNDER"

Psalm ii: 3

22945

186

22945

N⁰ 42. – RECITATIVE FOR TENOR

"He that dwelleth in heaven"

N⁰ 43. – AIR FOR TENOR

"Thou shalt break them"

22945

Thou shalt dash them in piec - es like a pot - - ter's

ves - sel, Thou shalt dash them in piec - es, in

cresc.

piec - es like a pot -

- ter's ves - sel.

B

Thou shalt break them,

*) Händel in his score has this
section in unison

22945

pot - - -ter's ves - sel, Thou shalt dash them in

pieces like a pot - - - ter's

D

ves - sel.

Nº 44.– CHORUS
"Hallelujah!"

Rev. xix: 6; xi: 15; xix: 16

*) Händel's score has one 8th note e here only; see foot-note on next page.

*) Händel's score has here 2 syllables for one note, it is therefore better to substitute two 16th notes for the 8th

198

22945

199

22945

END OF PART II

PART III

Nº 45.- AIR FOR SOPRANO

"I KNOW THAT MY REDEEMER LIVETH"

Job xix; 25, 26; 1 Cor. xv: 20

*) This appeggiatura is not in Händel's score

stand _____ at the lat - - - ter day up - on the earth,

up - on __ the earth:

D

And though worms de - stroy this bod - y,

yet in my flesh shall I see

cresc.

know that my Re - deem - er liv - eth.

For now is Christ ris-en from the dead,

the first - - fruits of them that

sleep, _____ of them that sleep, the

first - -fruits of them that sleep.

№ 46. – CHORUS

"Since by man came death"

1 Cor. xv: 21

N⁰ 47. – RECITATIVE FOR BASS
"Behold, I tell you a mystery"

1 Cor. xv: 51, 52

Be-hold, I tell you a mys-ter-y; we shall not all sleep, but we shall all be chang'd in a mo-ment, in the twinkling of an eye, at the last trumpet.

N⁰ 48. – AIR FOR BASS
"The trumpet shall sound"

1 Cor. xv: 52, 53

Pomposo, ma non allegro (♩=80)

Trumpet Solo

BASS SOLO

The trum-pet shall sound, _____ and the dead shall be

raised, and the dead shall be raised _____ in-cor-

rup-ti-ble; the

trum-pet shall sound, and the dead shall be raised, be raised in - cor - rup-ti-ble, be raised in - cor - rup-ti-ble, and we shall be chang'd, and we shall be chang'd.

*) Händel's score has here in-cor-rup-ti-ble

**) Händel's score has here, including last note in preceding bar, in-cor-rup-ti-ble

23945

For this cor - rup - ti-ble must put on in - - cor - rup-tion,

for this cor - rup-ti-ble must put on,

must put on,

__ must put on, must put on in - - cor - rup-tion;

and this mor - tal must put __ on im-mor-

*) This section is generally omitted.
22945

Nọ 49. - RECITATIVE FOR ALTO
"THEN SHALL BE BROUGHT TO PASS"

1 Cor. xv: 54

Then shall be brought to pass the say-ing that is writ-ten, Death is swal-low'd up in vic-to-ry.

*) Nos. 49, 50, 51, 52 are generally omitted.

Nọ 50. - DUET FOR ALTO AND TENOR
"O DEATH, WHERE IS THY STING?"

1 Cor. xv: 55, 56

O death, O death, where, where is thy sting? O death, where is thy sting? O grave, where, where is thy vic-to-ry? O grave!

O grave, O grave, where, where is thy vic-to-ry? where is thy vic-to-ry? O death,

N.B. — This Duet is given in the abridged form indicated by Händel in the Dublin score. Compare the Full Score.

Nº 51. – CHORUS
"But thanks be to God"

1 Cor. xv: 57

№ 52.- AIR FOR SOPRANO
"IF GOD BE FOR US, WHO CAN BE AGAINST US?"

Romans viii: 31,33,34

Larghetto (♩=88)

A SOPRANO *) SOLO

If God be for us, who can be a-

gainst us? who can be a - gainst us? who can be a -

*) Händel's score has here

If be a -

22945

gainst us?   If God be for us, who can be a-

gainst us?

B

Who shall lay an-y-thing to the charge of God's e-lect?

of God's e-lect?

Who shall lay an-y-thing to the charge

of God's e - lect?

C

It is God that

jus-ti - -fi-eth, it is God that jus-ti - fi - -

D

- eth.

Who is he that con-demneth?

who is he that con-demneth? who is

he that con-demn - - - - eth?

E

It is Christ that

di-ed, yea ra-ther, that is ris-en a-gain,

who is at the right hand of God, who makes in - ter - ces-sion for us, who makes in - ter - ces-sion for us, in - ter - ces - sion for us, who makes in - ter - ces - - - - sion, who makes in - ter-

ces - - - sion for us, who is at the

right hand of God, who is at the right hand of God, at the right hand of

Adagio

God, who makes in-ter - ces-sion for us.

ad lib.

f a tempo

N.º 53. – CHORUS

"Worthy is the Lamb that was slain"

Rev. v: 12,13

243

246

F Allegro moderato

F Allegro moderato (♩ = 88)

22945

CPSIA information can be obtained
at www.ICGtesting.com
Printed in the USA
LVHW010715141021
700295LV00001B/3

9 781297 496448